Stick It to the Boss!

by

S.J. Lippitt

Bloomington, IN  Milton Keynes, UK

authorHOUSE®

AuthorHouse™
1663 Liberty Drive, Suite 200
Bloomington, IN 47403
www.authorhouse.com
Phone: 1-800-839-8640

AuthorHouse™ UK Ltd.
500 Avebury Boulevard
Central Milton Keynes, MK9 2BE
www.authorhouse.co.uk
Phone: 08001974150

First published by AuthorHouse 4/9/2007

ISBN: 978-1-4259-6073-5 (sc)

Library of Congress Control Number: 2006910592

*Printed in the United States of America
Bloomington, Indiana*

This book is printed on acid-free paper.

This book is dedicated to the memory
of my uncle, Steven D. Baron.

To all of my bosses, without them this book could never have been written.

1

Say hello to everyone.

Remember that you weren't always rich and powerful.

3

If you have meetings scheduled with employees, don't forget about them.

4

Giving compliments will make accepting criticism much easier to handle.

5

Don't always talk business; people have lives outside of work.

6

If work is slow and you don't need the full workforce, let a few people have the day off.

7

Remember, your employees always think you are talking about them; your attitude could dictate their whole day.

8

People need a break. Implement a reasonable vacation program..

9

Help people grow.

10

It's hard to succeed. Bottom line: don't forget that LUCK is part of it.

11

Let people know what's going on; employees usually know if they are being excluded.

12

People should work to live, not live to work.

13

If you have a criticism for an employee, don't confront them with it as they are walking out the door on the Friday before a long weekend.

14

Listen.

15

You may drive a fancy car to work (and that is great), but the people working for you don't need you to tell them all the details.

16

There is a difference between a vacation day and a personal day.

17

Successful employees don't always make great managers.

18

If any employee asks what you did over the weekend and you have the time to answer, have the courtesy to return the question in kind.

19

Get rid of the word "however."

20

Eye contact is very important.

21

Good coffee doesn't cost much.

22

Don't let paperwork be the reason for delaying a promotion.

23

Success feels good; make sure your employees feel it too.

24

If your company is successful, do not forget that it is your employees who comprise it.

25

Being hands-on is great, but you hired your employees to do this work. Let them do it—it will help them grow.

26

Don't hover.

27

Never schedule big meetings for the Friday before a holiday weekend.

28

If an employee has an idea, remember that the patent office hasn't closed yet.

29

If you are in a meeting with an employee that they have requested pay attention; the other stuff can wait a few more minutes.

30

Have a sense of humor.

31

If you give an employee a promotion, remember that they EARNED it. Don't make them feel like they owe you.

32

Promote from within.

33

A good manager doesn't need to constantly tell his or her employees how well he or she is managing..

34

Have casual Fridays.

Have diversity.

36

Don't complain to your employees about those annoying managerial tasks you have to do. That's part of being a manager.

Treat people in the same way you would want to be treated.

38

A career is a journey, not a final destination.

39

Never answer your phone during an employee meeting.

40

Ask for volunteers, don't assign them.

41

Opportunity—you were given it— don't forget to give it back.

42

Remember that everyone who works hard should also get to play hard.

43

If you have employees pick up your lunch, give them the money up front; don't make them ask for it.

44

If the same employee gets your lunch every day, buy that employee lunch at least once per month.

45

If you have been out of the office, make sure that you touch base with your employees and say hello when you get back; don't just sit in your office all day catching up on paperwork.

46

Be respectful.

47

Speak to your employees not at them.

48

Smile and laugh.

49

Have good benefits.

50

Always call your employees by their first names.

51

Compliment in public and criticize in private.

52

Face time does not equal productivity.

53

Fear is not a productive motivator.

54

Give credit where credit is due.

55

Always order extra customer gifts so your employees can enjoy them too.

56

Focus on the process and good people will be very productive; it is easy to blame people for a poor process. *

57

Be humble.

58

Even in tough times, keep the holiday party; it might be the only time your employees have to unwind.

59

Go to the holiday party; your appearance is crucial in many ways.

60

Every Friday should be a half day for at least half of the staff during the summer.

61

Encourage your employees to help define the corporate culture.

62

Recognize your employees' personal accomplishments.

63

Utilize your employees.

64

Be understanding, but don't be a pushover, your employees won't respect you.

65

If your employee has an idea, create an environment where they feel they can voice it.

66

Don't forget what it is like to work in the trenches.

67

Remember that small things go a long way.

68

If you assign an employee to work on a project, have the courtesy to appear at the presentation when they have finished it.

69

Time is valuable to your employees, too.

70

If you have a favorite employee, don't make it obvious.

71

Of course we work to feel accomplished, but it is also obvious that we work to get paid.

72

Remember—you are the boss; don't force your employees to make decisions that you should make.

73

Be Fair.

74

Don't forget the people who helped you get where you are.

75

Don't forget that you wouldn't be able to have the board meeting without the guy who maintains the boardroom and keeps your business running; you won't get far without power, phones, heat, plumbing, etc.

76

Don't forget that it is a lot easier to have people follow you than it is to lug dead weight.

Remember that every time you make a decision, you are setting a precedent.

78

If you are running your family business, remember that you weren't necessarily the one who built it.

79

Just because someone is your friend doesn't mean that he or she will make a good manager or employee.

80

Don't make your employees travel or entertain more than the job requires; their families will thank you and your clients will appreciate their visits more if they have something new to discuss.

81

Revenues are important, but happy employees are, too.

82

Family should come first.

83

Never show favoritism in public.

84

Make all financial deals crystal clear before your people begin to produce; don't change things after the fact.

85

Pizza on a Friday.

86

Do what you love.

87

Everyone likes to feel good.

88

Be aware of your employees. Pay attention to the changes in their lives, their families, and their appearances; congratulate them on a new home, baby, etc.

89

Be genuine.

90

A birthday list is always a plus.

91

Knowing people's names and what they do for your company is essential.

92

Always remember that everything you say and do counts.

93

Encourage people to be the best that they can be and to take chances to try and better themselves.

94

Be truthful.

95

Pay corporate expenses on time; don't make your employees fight to get the money back. Have a corporate card; most employees don't have a couple of thousand extra dollars lying around

96

Hold all employees to the same standard.

97

Don't talk to your employees about other employees; it's unprofessional, and trust me, most are smart enough to recognize that it is happening.

98

Recognize your employees' accomplishments in a way that gives every one of them a chance to succeed.

99

If you are going to schedule a meeting after work, give advance notice; don't tell people the day of the meeting.

100

Being respected is a lot harder then being loved.

When you get up and go to work, try to recite the words of my uncle, Steven Baron, one of the greatest managers and friends I have ever known: *"**If there is anything I can do for you, I have the time**."* Try to approach your job as a manager with this attitude. Steven signed all his correspondences with this phrase; it really sums up the approach that every manager should have.

*Based on the management theory of Edward Deming.

www.ingramcontent.com/pod-product-compliance
Lightning Source LLC
Chambersburg PA
CBHW020313290526
45784CB00003B/1500